Morning Mastery

Morning Mastery

101 morning habits to transform your day

ARUNA JOSHI

First Edition 2025,
Published in India by:
Embassy Book Distributors
120, Great Western Building, Maharashtra Chamber of
Commerce Lane, Fort, Mumbai 400 023, India
Tel: (+9122) -30967415, 22819546
Email: info@embassybooks.in
www.embassybooks.in

ISBN: 978-81-19729-79-1

Distribution Centres:
Mumbai, Ahmedabad, Bangalore, Kolkata, Chennai,
Hyderabad, New Delhi, Pune

Cover Design by Rishikumar Thakur for Embassy Book Distributors

Printed & bound in India by Thomson Press India Ltd.

Introduction

"You'll never change your life until you change something you do daily. The secret of your success is found in your daily routine." - ***John C. Maxwell***

Mornings are more than just the start of a new day—they are a golden opportunity to set the tone for everything that follows. Yet, in today's fast-paced and demanding world, mornings often feel chaotic and rushed, leaving us stressed before the day has even begun. But what if mornings could be different? What if they could become a powerful launchpad for productivity, happiness, and self-discovery?

As children, we often follow structured routines—a disciplined rhythm of waking up, studying, eating, playing, and sleeping. These routines aren't just habits; they are the foundation of our physical, mental, and emotional well-being. Yet, as we grow into adulthood, the structure fades, and gets replaced by the unpredictability of our fast-changing lives. We embrace spontaneity, believing it brings freedom and excitement, only to find ourselves battling stress, anxiety, and a sense of being unfulfilled.

This book, *Morning Mastery: 101 Morning Habits to Transform Your Day*, is an invitation to reclaim the magic of a structured, intentional start to the day. Drawing on research and practical insights, it reveals how designing and adhering to a morning routine can not only boost productivity but also unlock our true potential.

The 101 habits outlined in this book are simple yet transformative. From invigorating physical exercises that energize your body to mindfulness practices that calm your mind, these habits are designed to align with your unique lifestyle and goals. Whether it's beginning the day with a refreshing glass of water, stepping outside for a brisk walk, or taking a moment to reflect on your dreams, these small actions have the power to create profound change.

This is not a one-size-fits-all approach. Instead, this book encourages you to explore and experiment with the habits, discovering what resonates with you and fits seamlessly into your life. The goal isn't to adopt every habit but to craft a morning routine that feels authentic, empowering, and uniquely yours.

A thoughtfully planned morning doesn't just shape the hours ahead—it influences who we are and who we can become. A well-designed routine provides the discipline, clarity, and energy to chase our goals, live with intention, and find joy in the everyday.

This book is for anyone—busy professionals, students, parents, or anyone seeking balance—who wishes to transform their mornings into a time of growth and inspiration. By embracing these habits, you will take the first steps toward a life of greater freedom, fulfilment, and purpose.

Let this book be your guide to designing mornings that empower you to rise, shine, and thrive.

Wake Up Early

Give yourself extra time for a calm start

Waking up early offers a powerful way to start your day with calm, purpose, and control. By giving yourself extra time, you create a buffer between waking up and daily demands, allowing you to set a steady, unhurried pace. Early risers often enjoy reduced stress, greater clarity, and a sense of accomplishment that comes from being in control of their mornings.

Drink a Glass of Water

Rehydrate to energize and boost metabolism

Starting your day with a glass of water is a simple yet impactful habit that supports your body in countless ways. After a night's sleep, your body is naturally dehydrated and in need of replenishment. Drinking water first thing in the morning helps kickstart your metabolism, promoting better digestion and more efficient calorie burning throughout the day. It also assists in flushing out toxins that accumulate overnight, clearing the way for improved skin health and an energy boost that will leave you feeling refreshed and alert. This small act of hydration can have an uplifting effect on mood and focus, setting the stage for a productive and energized day ahead.

Stretch Your Body

Loosen up muscles and improve circulation

Starting your morning with a good stretch can do wonders for your body and mind. When we are sleeping in the night, our muscles tend to stiffen due to inactivity. Stretching helps loosen them up, increases flexibility and reduces any stiffness or aches. A few minutes of stretching improves blood flow, which helps deliver oxygen and nutrients throughout your body, creating a sense of alertness and energy. Beyond the physical benefits, stretching can also enhance mental clarity and provide a calming effect, helping you ease into the day with less stress. This gentle start to your morning aligns both body and mind, creating a foundation of relaxation and readiness for whatever the day brings.

Practice Gratitude

List three things you are thankful for

Practicing gratitude each morning is a simple but powerful way to set a positive tone for your day. Take a moment and list three things you are thankful for each morning as soon as you wake up. Doing this shifts your focus from what might be lacking to what you already have, nurturing a mindset of abundance. Whether it's the comfort of a home, the support of loved ones, or even something as simple as a sunny day, acknowledging these blessings brings in a sense of appreciation and joy. Research shows that regularly practicing gratitude can reduce stress, and improve overall well-being. This daily ritual not only uplifts your mood, enabling you to approach each day with a positive perspective.

Mindful Breathing

Try five minutes of deep breathing for focus

Practicing mindful breathing for just five minutes each morning is an excellent way to centre yourself and enhance focus for the day ahead. Deep breathing involves inhaling slowly, holding, and exhaling fully, which triggers the body's relaxation response and reduces stress. This practice delivers more oxygen to the brain, which promotes mental clarity and prepares you for focused, thoughtful action.

Read an Inspiring Quote

Set a positive tonewith wise words

Wise words often render deep truths or new perspectives that help shift our mindset. Reading an inspiring quote in the morning can be a powerful way to set a positive tone for the day ahead. It can uplift, motivate, or even spark creativity, providing a fresh outlook on any challenges we may face. Keep a quotes book handy and read a quote before you kick-start your day. This simple habit can help you feel more grounded, optimistic, and ready to tackle whatever comes your way.

Morning Walk

Enjoy nature or fresh air to wake up your senses

A morning walk is a rejuvenating way to awaken your senses and start the day feeling refreshed. Stepping outside and breathing in fresh air while moving your body helps to boost circulation and lift your mood, providing an instant sense of clarity and vitality. Walking in nature offers a welcome break from screens and other indoor distractions, allowing you to soak in the beauty and stillness of your surroundings. This exposure to natural light also helps regulate your circadian rhythm, making you feel more alert in the morning and improving sleep at night. A morning walk gives a calm yet energizing start to the day, creating space for reflection.

Cold Shower

Boost circulation and increase alertness

Starting your day with a cold shower might sound daunting, but it's an invigorating way to boost circulation and sharpen your focus. The shock of cold water prompts blood to flow to your organs and muscles, improving circulation and oxygen delivery, which can leave you feeling more awake and energized. Although cold showers may be a bit discomforting in the beginning, but the benefits are numerous.

Journal Your Goals

Write down what you want to accomplish

Journaling your goals is a powerful practice that can transform your aspirations into actionable steps. By taking the time to write down what you want to accomplish, you create a clear roadmap that clarifies your intentions and helps you stay focused on your objectives. This act of writing not only solidifies your commitment but also allows you to break down larger goals into manageable tasks, making them feel more attainable. Additionally, revisiting your goals regularly can inspire motivation and reflection, enabling you to track your progress and make necessary adjustments along the way.

Visualize Success

Picture positive outcomes for your day

Visualizing success is about mentally stepping into a world where your day unfolds in exactly the way you hope. Set aside a few minutes in the morning and sit in a place where no one will disturb you, with your eyes closed. Visualize exactly how you want your day to pass. See yourself embracing challenges with confidence, your goals taking shape smoothly, and each interaction bringing mutual positivity. Picture yourself completing tasks with ease and satisfaction, and notice the feeling of accomplishment that follows. This habit of visualization not only reduces anxiety but boosts self-confidence, making it more likely that your day will reflect the vision you have created.

Eat a Nutritious Breakfast

Fuel your body with balanced energy

Starting your day with a nutritious breakfast is one of the simplest yet most powerful ways to fuel your body and mind. A balanced breakfast, rich in protein, fibre, and healthy fats, provides steady energy, helping you stay focused and alert throughout the morning. Nourishing your body with a good breakfast in the morning helps prevent energy crashes that lead to cravings. Whether it's a bowl of oatmeal topped with nuts and berries, a smoothie packed with greens and protein, or whole-grain toast with avocado, a good breakfast gives you the boost needed to tackle your day with vigour.

Set Intentions

Choose a value or goal to guide your day

Setting intentions gives your day direction and purpose, aligning your actions with what truly matters to you. Intentions encourage you to make conscious choices that reflect your aspirations, helping you stay grounded even when distractions arise. Unlike a rigid to-do list, an intention is adaptable, allowing you to recalibrate as needed. By starting each day with a clear intention, you set a foundation for living purposefully and mindfully.

Limit Screen Time

Avoid screens for the first 30 minutes

Limiting screen time for the first 30 minutes of your day can be transformative. It helps you stay focused on the day ahead before diving into the demands of the digital world. This screen-free period lets you slide into your morning routines smoothly. Without the immediate barrage of notifications, emails, and social media updates, you give yourself space to fully wake up and mentally prepare. This small practice helps reduce stress, improve focus, and creates a calmer mindset, allowing you to approach the rest of your day with clarity and purpose.

Listen to Uplifting Music

Start your day with motivating tunes

Starting your day with uplifting music is a simple yet powerful way to set a positive tone and boost your mood. Energizing tunes, whether they're rhythmic beats, inspiring lyrics, Mantra chanting or any soulful melodies can instantly lift your spirits and bring motivation. Music taps into our emotions, helping to shake off sleepiness and set an optimistic mindset. Playing your favourite feel-good tracks can become a morning ritual, filling you with enthusiasm and inspiring you to take on the day's challenges.

Quick Yoga Session

Stretch and strengthen for a balanced start

A quick yoga session in the morning is a fantastic way to awaken both body and mind, offering a great start to your day. Through simple stretches and poses, you gently release tension, increase flexibility, and invigorate your muscles, preparing you for whatever lies ahead. A few sets of pranayama helps calm the mind, creating a sense of inner peace and clarity that grounds you for the day.

Smile in the Mirror

Boost your mood with a quick smile

Starting your day with a smile in the mirror is a small, simple act with a big impact on your mood. Smiling releases feel-good hormones like serotonin and dopamine, instantly lifting your spirits. By looking at yourself and smiling, you're giving yourself a moment of positive affirmation, boosting confidence and self-compassion. It also acts as a reminder to face whatever comes with positivity, turning a simple glance in the mirror into a powerful mood booster and a source of inner encouragement.

Organize Your Space

A tidy environment boosts focus

Organizing your space is a powerful way to clear mental clutter and boost your focus. A tidy environment, free of unnecessary distractions, allows your mind to settle and concentrate on the tasks at hand. Whether it's your desk, room, or workspace, taking a few minutes to organize creates a sense of order and control that translates to a calmer, more productive mindset. When everything is in its place, you will find it easier to access what you need and stay on track, avoiding the misplacement of items leading to chaos. A clean space sets the stage for clear thinking, making it easier to accomplish your goals and feel a sense of accomplishment.

Meditate

Spend a few minutes in mindfulness

Spending a few minutes in meditation each morning can transform your entire day by grounding you in mindfulness and clarity. Meditation helps centre your thoughts, reduce stress, and enhance emotional resilience, making you more equipped to handle whatever comes your way. Even just a few minutes of mindfulness creates space between you and the day's challenges, helping you feel more in control and in the present moment. Starting your day with this practice sets a foundation of peace and purpose.

Review Your To-Do List

Organize tasksfor the day

Reviewing your to-do list each morning is a powerful way to bring structure and intention to your day. By organizing tasks in order of priority, you gain a clear sense of direction, making it easier to stay focused and efficient. This quick review also helps you anticipate challenges, set realistic goals, and avoid feeling overwhelmed. A well-thought-out list provides a roadmap, ensuring that your energy is spent on what matters most. Starting the day with this step creates momentum, empowering you to tackle each item with purpose and keeping you motivated as you check things off throughout the day.

Enjoy Coffee or Tea Mindfully

Savor each sip without distractions

Enjoying your coffee or tea mindfully is a delightful ritual that enhances your morning experience and fosters a sense of calm. Take a moment to savour each sip, fully engaging your senses as you appreciate the aroma, warmth, and flavour. By setting aside distractions—like your phone or TV—you create a peaceful space to enjoy this simple pleasure, allowing your mind to relax and be present. This mindful practice not only promotes relaxation but also helps cultivate gratitude for the little moments in life.

Practice Sun Salutations

Wake up body and mind with yoga

Start your day with Sun Salutations to awaken both body and mind, setting a positive tone for the hours ahead. This flowing sequence of yoga postures, commonly known as Surya Namaskar, stretches and energizes every muscle, activating circulation and promoting flexibility. As you move through each posture with mindful breathing, you're not only working your body but also focusing your mind, cultivating calm and clarity. Practicing Sun Salutations in the morning aligns you with nature's rhythm, inviting a sense of peace and readiness to embrace whatever the day brings.

Morning Affirmations

Say positive phrases to empower yourself

Start each day with empowering affirmations to set a positive, purposeful tone. Morning affirmations—simple, uplifting phrases like "I am the best," "Today is full of opportunity," or "I approach each moment with gratitude"—can create a mindset of positivity and confidence. By saying these phrases aloud or repeating them in your mind, you reshape your thoughts, anchoring yourself in positivity and self-belief. This daily ritual can go a long way in empowering you in every way.

Create a Mini Exercise Routine

Push-ups, jumping jacks, or squats

Kick-start your day with a quick mini exercise routine to boost energy and elevate your mood. Incorporate simple moves like push-ups, jumping jacks, or squats—each one works a different muscle group, helping you build strength, increase endurance, and improve balance. A short burst of exercise in the morning stimulates circulation, wakes up your muscles, and releases feel-good endorphins. This routine doesn't require any equipment and can be done in just a few minutes, making it easy to fit into any schedule. A few minutes of movement can have a powerful impact, setting you up for a day filled with focus and vitality.

Plan Tomorrow Today

Note a few priorities for the next day

End your day by setting a clear path for tomorrow with a quick note of your top priorities. Jotting down a few key tasks or goals helps you start the next day with focus and purpose, reducing the mental clutter that can come with unfinished to-dos. This simple habit allows you to reflect on what truly matters and plan your time effectively. By organizing your thoughts in advance, you create a sense of direction that guides you through the day, helping you stay on track and manage your energy. Letting tomorrow's priorities rest on paper can also bring a sense of closure, allowing you to unwind and enjoy a more restful night's sleep.

Declutter a Small Area

Clear a desk or counterto feel organized

Take a few moments to declutter a small area, like your desk or kitchen counter, to invite a sense of order and calm into your day. Clearing away unnecessary items not only creates a tidy space but also helps free your mind from distractions, making it easier to focus. This small act of organization can have a surprisingly big impact on your mood, offering a fresh start and a feeling of accomplishment. A clutter-free area allows you to feel more in control of your environment and encourages a productive, stress-free mindset. Small, manageable steps like this can make a difference, inspiring you to keep a sense of clarity and simplicity throughout your day.

Connect with Loved Ones

Share a message or quick call

Take a few minutes each day to connect with loved ones—a quick message or call can brighten both your day and theirs. In our busy lives, small gestures like sending a thoughtful text, sharing a funny moment, or making a brief call can go a long way in maintaining meaningful relationships. This habit nurtures bonds, brings warmth to your heart, and reminds you of the support and love surrounding you. Such connections also provide a comforting sense of belonging, grounding you and lifting your spirits. Staying connected, even in small ways, is a simple yet powerful way to keep relationships strong and bring joy to your daily routine. The commuting time to work can be effectively used for this purpose.

Mindful Shower

Enjoy the sensations and let it refresh you

Transform your daily shower into a mindful experience, allowing yourself to fully savour the sensations of warmth, water, and relaxation. As you stand under the spray, pay attention to the feel of the water on your skin, the scent of your soap, and the gentle rhythm of your breathing. Let the shower wash away stress and refresh your mind, helping you feel grounded and cantered. This short ritual brings you instantly to the present moment, calming any racing thoughts and bringing a moment of peace.

Breathe in Fresh Scents

Try essential oils for a calming effect

Aromas like lavender, eucalyptus, or citrus can have an immediate calming effect, easing stress and uplifting your mood. Place a few drops on a cloth, use a diffuser, or simply inhale from the bottle, letting the scent fill your senses. Essential oils work with your mind and body, helping to enhance focus, reduce anxiety, or promote relaxation, depending on the aroma you choose. This simple practice can transform your space and mind, offering a sensory retreat that helps you feel grounded and refreshed.

Take Deep Breaths

Calm your mind with rhythmic breathing

Calm your mind and body with the simple yet powerful act of deep breathing. Taking slow, rhythmic breaths—inhale deeply through your nose, hold for a moment, and then exhale fully—can help you release tension, ease anxiety, and bring a sense of balance. This mindful breathing practice activates your body's natural relaxation response, slowing your heart rate and calming your nervous system. By focusing on each breath, you also quiet any racing thoughts, allowing your mind to feel more cantered and clear. Just a few minutes of deep breathing can create a peaceful pause, helping you approach the rest of your day with calm and clarity.

Practice Progressive Muscle Relaxation

Ease into the day tension-free

Start your day tension-free with a simple progressive muscle relaxation exercise, easing both body and mind into a calm state. This technique involves gradually tensing, holding, and then relaxing each muscle group, starting from your toes and working up to your head. As you consciously release the tension in each area, you may notice stress melting away, replaced by a sense of warmth and ease. Progressive muscle relaxation not only relieves physical tightness but also encourages mental relaxation, grounding you in the present moment. Put on some nice relaxing music to make the process more effective and enjoyable. This gentle routine is a powerful tool for reducing stress, helping you greet the day with a refreshed body and a peaceful mind.

Step Outside for Sunshine

Boost your mood with natural light

Step outside and soak up some sunshine to give your mood an instant boost. Natural light helps your body produce vitamin D, which supports overall health and can significantly improve your energy and outlook. A few minutes outdoors, breathing fresh air and feeling the warmth of the sun on your skin, can reduce stress and elevate your mood. Sunlight exposure also regulates your body's internal clock, helping you feel more awake during the day and promoting better sleep at night. Taking this small break to connect with nature can be a refreshing way to recharge, helping you feel balanced and ready for whatever the day holds.

Journal Your Thoughts

Clear mental clutter with free writing

Set aside a few minutes to journal your thoughts, allowing yourself to release mental clutter and gain clarity. Free writing—putting down whatever comes to mind without judgment or structure—can be incredibly freeing, helping you process emotions, explore ideas, and reflect on your day. By putting your thoughts on paper, you create space in your mind, making it easier to focus and feel calm. Journaling can also reveal patterns, insights, and new perspectives that might otherwise go unnoticed. This simple habit is a powerful tool for self-discovery and relaxation, leaving you with a clearer mind and a lighter heart.

Plan a Self-Care Activity

Add something enjoyable to your day

Intentionally plan a self-care activity to bring joy and relaxation into your day. Whether it's a favourite hobby, a walk in nature, a warm bath, a massage, or time to read, adding something you genuinely enjoy can boost your mood and replenish your energy. Taking this time for yourself isn't just about indulgence; it's about honoring your needs and well-being. Including a small moment of self-care helps create balance, reminding you to nurture yourself amidst life's demands. This simple act of prioritizing joy can be uplifting, helping you approach the rest of your day with a renewed sense of positivity and resilience.

Read a Motivating Book

Start with an inspiring chapter

Dedicate a few minutes to reading a motivating book, starting with a chapter that inspires and uplifts you. Engaging with positive, insightful content can shift your perspective, spark new ideas, and even fuel your determination. When you immerse yourself in an encouraging story or valuable lesson, you connect with the author's wisdom and experiences, reminding you that growth and resilience are within reach. This daily dose of inspiration not only boosts your mood but also equips you with practical tools and encouragement to face challenges. A small habit of reading motivation can set a powerful tone, empowering you to carry positivity into every part of your day.

Try a Creative Hobby

Sketch, write, or play an instrument

Engage in a creative hobby to bring a sense of joy and expression to your day—whether it's sketching, writing, playing an instrument, or any other form of art that calls to you. Creative activities allow you to connect with your inner self, channelling thoughts and emotions into something tangible and uniquely yours. This time spent in creativity can be therapeutic, reducing stress and enhancing focus as you immerse yourself in the process. A creative hobby is also a wonderful way to explore new skills, challenge yourself, and experience the thrill of making something meaningful. This small practice can brighten your day, boost your mood, and add a fulfilling sense of accomplishment.

Create a 'Do Not Disturb' Zone

Carve out uninterrupted time

Designate a 'Do Not Disturb' zone to gift yourself uninterrupted, focused time each day. This space—whether a physical room, a desk, or a set time frame—is free from distractions, allowing you to fully immerse in tasks, creativity, or simply quiet reflection. By setting boundaries with devices, notifications, and interruptions, you cultivate an environment where you can concentrate, recharge, and connect deeply with your work or relaxation. This dedicated zone not only enhances productivity but also reduces stress, as you know you'll have time set aside to attend to important tasks without disruptions. This practice can create balance and mindfulness in a busy world, helping you feel more in control.

Mindful Eating

SFocus on your food's taste and texture

Practice mindful eating by fully engaging with your food's taste, texture, and aroma, savouring each bite with intention. Instead of eating on autopilot or multitasking, take the time to appreciate the flavours and textures on your plate. Chew slowly, noticing the variety of tastes, and let yourself truly enjoy the experience of nourishing your body. This simple shift in awareness can turn a meal into a moment of calm, reducing stress and enhancing satisfaction. Mindful eating not only promotes better digestion but also helps you develop a healthier, more balanced relationship with food. By focusing on the present moment, you bring a sense of gratitude and enjoyment to every meal.

Do a Brain Puzzle

Wake up your mind with a challenge

Engage your mind with a brain puzzle to awaken your cognitive abilities and start your day with a stimulating challenge. Whether it's a crossword, Sudoku, or a logic puzzle, these activities not only provide entertainment but also enhance your problem-solving skills and mental agility. Taking just a few minutes to tackle a puzzle can sharpen your focus, boost creativity, and improve memory as you train your brain to think critically. This fun mental workout serves as a refreshing way to jumpstart your day, energizing your mind and preparing you for the tasks ahead. Embracing this habit can create a positive momentum, inspiring you to approach the rest of your day with enthusiasm and clarity.

Set a Personal Goal

A small win builds motivation

Set a personal goal each day, focusing on a small win that can boost your motivation and sense of accomplishment. Whether it's finishing a book chapter, completing a workout, or organizing a cluttered space, achieving these manageable objectives can create a powerful ripple effect in your life. By breaking larger aspirations into smaller, attainable steps, you build momentum and reinforce your self-discipline, making it easier to tackle bigger challenges over time. Celebrating these small victories not only enhances your confidence but also cultivates a positive mindset, propelling you forward and encouraging you to continue striving for growth and success.

Mindful Listening

Listen to birds, music, or a podcast

Embrace the art of mindful listening by tuning into the sounds around you—whether it's the gentle chirping of birds, your favourite music, or an engaging podcast. This practice invites you to fully immerse yourself in auditory experiences, allowing each sound to wash over you and capture your attention. By focusing on the nuances of rhythm, melody, or spoken words, you cultivate a deeper connection to the present moment and enhance your awareness of the world around you. Mindful listening not only promotes relaxation but also transforms even the simplest moments into meaningful experiences. This intentional practice can provide a refreshing break from daily distractions, grounding you and helping you find peace amidst life's noise.

Reflect on a Positive Memory

Revisit a happy moment for joy

Take a moment to reflect on a positive memory, revisiting a happy moment that brings you joy and warmth. Close your eyes and allow yourself to immerse in the details of that experience—the sights, sounds, and feelings that made it special. Whether it's a joyful family gathering, a personal achievement, or a spontaneous adventure, recalling these treasured moments can evoke feelings of gratitude and contentment. This simple practice not only uplifts your mood but also reinforces a sense of hope and resilience, reminding you of the beauty and happiness that life offers. By regularly reflecting on positive memories, you create a reservoir of joy that can inspire you during challenging times, helping you maintain a more optimistic outlook on life.

Make Your Bed

This small win starts your day with order

Start your day on a positive note by making your bed—a simple yet powerful habit that instils a sense of order and accomplishment. Taking a few moments to tidy your sleeping space not only creates a visually pleasing environment but also sets a productive tone for the rest of your day. This small win can boost your motivation and reinforce the mindset that you are capable of achieving more. When you return home, a neatly made bed can provide a calming sense of completion, reminding you that even in the midst of chaos, you have the power to create order. Embracing this simple routine can foster a sense of discipline and clarity, laying the foundation for a more organized and focused day ahead.

Find a Morning Mantra

Repeat a calming or empowering phrase

Begin each day by finding a morning mantra that resonates with you, a calming or empowering phrase that sets a positive intention for the hours ahead. Repeating this mantra—whether it's "I am strong and capable" or "I embrace today with gratitude"—can help centre your thoughts and focus your energy. By incorporating a mantra into your morning routine, you create a powerful affirmation that can boost your confidence and inspire you to face the day with clarity and purpose. This intentional act of self-empowerment not only enhances your mood but also reinforces your belief in your own potential, guiding you toward a more fulfilling day.

Review Your Long-Term Goals

Reflect on your "why"

Take time to review your long-term goals and reflect on your underlying "why"—the deeper motivations that drive your aspirations. Understanding the reasons behind your goals not only strengthens your commitment but also provides clarity and direction as you navigate life's challenges. By reconnecting with your core values and desires, you remind yourself of the purpose behind your efforts, fostering resilience and determination. This reflection can illuminate any necessary adjustments to your path, ensuring that your actions align with your true aspirations. Regularly revisiting your long-term goals helps maintain focus and inspires you to stay dedicated to your vision, creating a sense of fulfilment as you work towards building the life you truly want.

Organize a Morning Playlist

Set a soundtrack for your day

Curate a morning playlist to set the perfect soundtrack for your day, enhancing your mood and energizing your routine. Select songs that inspire, uplift, and motivate you—whether they are upbeat tracks that make you want to dance or calming melodies that promote focus and serenity. Listening to a thoughtfully crafted playlist as you go through your morning rituals can create a positive atmosphere, making even mundane tasks feel more enjoyable. Music has the power to influence emotions and boost creativity, helping you start the day on a high note. By organizing a morning playlist, you not only infuse your routine with joy and energy but also cultivate a mindful experience that resonates throughout the day.

Practice Patience

Try to approach tasks calmly and mindfully

Cultivating patience is essential for approaching tasks calmly and mindfully, allowing you to navigate daily challenges with grace and resilience. Instead of rushing through activities or reacting impulsively, take a moment to breathe deeply and ground yourself in the present moment. This practice helps to clear your mind, enabling you to focus on the task at hand without the distraction of anxiety or frustration. By embracing patience, you create space for thoughtful reflection, improving decision-making and fostering a sense of control over your actions. This mindful approach not only enhances productivity but also promotes a more positive mindset, encouraging you to savour the process rather than fixating solely on the outcome. With each moment of patience, you reinforce the belief that it is okay to take your time, leading to greater satisfaction and fulfilment in your daily life.

Embrace Silence

Take a few minutes in quiet reflection

Embrace the power of silence by dedicating a few minutes each day to quiet reflection. In our fast-paced world, these moments of stillness offer a precious opportunity to pause, breathe, and connect with your inner self. Find a comfortable space, close your eyes, and allow your thoughts to settle as you tune into the sounds of your breath or the gentle rhythm of your heartbeat. This practice can help clear mental clutter, reduce stress, and foster a deeper understanding of your feelings and aspirations. By embracing silence, you create a sanctuary for introspection, allowing insights and creativity to emerge naturally. This simple yet profound ritual not only nurtures your well-being but also enhances your ability to respond thoughtfully to the world around you, making space for clarity and peace in your busy life.

Stand or Stretch

A quick stretch keeps energy flowing

Take a moment to stretch throughout your day, as a quick stretch can invigorate your body and keep energy flowing. Whether you are sitting at a desk or engaged in other tasks, incorporating short stretching breaks can relieve tension, improve circulation, and enhance focus. Simple movements, like reaching your arms overhead, rolling your shoulders, or gently bending forward, can rejuvenate your muscles and refresh your mind. These brief pauses help counteract the physical strain of prolonged sitting. By making stretching a regular part of your routine, you foster a sense of vitality and well-being, ensuring that you remain energized and engaged throughout your day.

Engage with a Pet

Bonding with animals can boost mood

Engaging with a pet is a wonderful way to boost your mood and foster a deep sense of connection. Spending time with animals—whether it is playing, cuddling, or simply observing their playful antics—can bring immense joy and comfort. The unconditional love and companionship they offer can reduce stress, alleviate anxiety, and enhance overall well-being. Pets have a unique ability to live in the moment, reminding us to slow down and appreciate the simple pleasures in life. The act of petting a dog or cat can release oxytocin, a hormone that promotes bonding and feelings of happiness. By making time to engage with your pet, you not only strengthen your bond but also create moments of joy and laughter that enrich your day, helping to cultivate a positive and nurturing environment.

Read a Poem

A poem can spark inspiration and beauty

Reading a poem can be a delightful way to spark inspiration and immerse yourself in beauty. The carefully crafted words and imagery can evoke emotions, provoke thought, and transport you to different worlds, all within just a few lines. Poetry has a unique ability to distil complex feelings and experiences into concise expressions, making it a powerful tool for reflection and introspection. Whether it's a classic sonnet or a contemporary piece, engaging with poetry encourages you to pause, contemplate, and connect with the essence of human experience. This brief escape into the world of words can ignite your creativity, soothe your mind, and leave you feeling uplifted, reminding you of the profound beauty that language can convey. Taking a moment to read a poem can enrich your day and inspire you to see the world through a more poetic lens.

Plan Leisure Time

Schedule something enjoyable

Make it a priority to plan leisure time by scheduling activities that bring you joy and relaxation. Whether it's a weekend outing, a cozy evening with a book, or a fun gathering with friends, intentionally setting aside time for enjoyable pursuits can significantly enhance your overall well-being. This dedicated leisure time allows you to recharge, fostering creativity and reducing stress in your daily life. By treating these moments as important appointments, you create a balance between productivity and enjoyment, ensuring that you nurture your passions and hobbies. Planning leisure time not only provides something to look forward to but also serves as a reminder of the importance of self-care and fulfilment.

Do a Quick Financial Check

Check budgets or track expenses

Conducting a quick financial check is a vital practice that can help you maintain control over your budget and track your expenses effectively. Setting aside just a few minutes to review your finances allows you to gain clarity on your spending habits and assess whether you are on track to meet your financial goals. By examining your budget, you can identify areas where you may need to cut back or adjust your spending, ensuring that you are living within your means. This proactive approach not only helps prevent financial stress but also empowers you to make informed decisions about your money. Regular financial check-ins cultivate a sense of accountability and awareness, enabling you to navigate your financial landscape with confidence and peace of mind. Embracing this simple habit can lead to greater financial stability and a more secure future.

Connect to Your Breathing

Deep breaths calm and centre you

Connecting to your breathing is a powerful practice that can bring calm and cantering to your mind and body. Taking a moment to focus on your breath allows you to slow down and cultivate mindfulness, helping to alleviate stress and anxiety. Deep, intentional breaths—inhale through your nose, allowing your abdomen to expand, and exhale slowly through your mouth—can activate your body's relaxation response, promoting a sense of peace and clarity. This simple act of awareness creates a space for reflection and grounding, reminding you to be present in the moment. By integrating breathwork into your daily routine, you not only enhance your mental well-being but also improve your overall health.

Practice Self-Compassion

Remind yourself it's okay to be imperfect

Practicing self-compassion is essential for nurturing a positive relationship with yourself, reminding you that it's perfectly okay to be imperfect. In a world that often emphasizes success and perfection, embracing your flaws and mistakes fosters a healthier mindset and emotional resilience. Instead of being critical or harsh when you face setbacks, treat yourself with the same kindness and understanding you would offer a close friend. Acknowledge that everyone experiences challenges and makes mistakes; it's a fundamental part of the human experience. By allowing yourself to feel vulnerable and accepting your imperfections, you create space for growth, healing, and self-acceptance. This gentle practice can reduce feelings of inadequacy and anxiety, helping you cultivate a more loving and forgiving attitude toward yourself. Ultimately, self-compassion empowers you to navigate life's ups and downs with grace and understanding, paving the way for a more fulfilling and joyful existence.

Write Down Priorities

Keep a few big goals top of mind

Writing down your priorities is a powerful strategy for keeping your most important goals top of mind. By clearly outlining your objectives, you create a tangible reference that serves as a constant reminder of what truly matters to you. This practice not only enhances focus but also helps you allocate your time and energy more effectively. Regularly reviewing your priorities encourages you to stay aligned with your values and intentions, making it easier to make decisions that support your goals. Additionally, having your priorities written down can reduce feelings of overwhelm, as it simplifies your tasks into manageable steps. By consciously tracking your progress and reflecting on your priorities, you cultivate a sense of purpose and direction, empowering you to take meaningful action toward achieving your aspirations. This intentional approach to goal-setting can transform your daily routine, allowing you to live with clarity and intention.

Practice Sunlight Meditation

Let light inspire positivity

Find a comfortable spot where you can bask in the warm glow of the sun, allowing its rays to envelop you as you settle into a state of calm. As you close your eyes, take deep breaths, and visualize the sunlight filling your body with warmth and energy. Imagine it dissolving any negativity or stress, replacing it with feelings of joy and tranquillity. This simple practice can invigorate your senses helping you cultivate a more positive outlook on life. By integrating this radiant ritual into your routine, you invite light and positivity to flow into your day, nurturing your well-being.

Do Something Unusual

Change a routine element for novelty

By breaking away from the mundane and introducing an unexpected element—whether it's taking a different route to work, trying a new recipe, or engaging in a spontaneous activity—you stimulate your mind and awaken your senses. This simple shift can spark creativity, inspire new ideas, and enhance your overall mood by providing a break from the familiar. Embracing novelty encourages you to step outside your comfort zone, fostering a spirit of adventure and openness to new experiences. Even small changes can have a profound impact, reminding you that life is full of possibilities and encouraging a mindset of curiosity.

Read a Motivational Story

Find a real story to inspire you

Reading a motivational story can be a powerful source of inspiration, allowing you to connect with the triumphs and challenges of others. These real-life narratives often highlight the resilience of the human spirit, showcasing individuals who have overcome adversity to achieve their dreams. Whether it's a tale of a groundbreaking entrepreneur, an athlete who defied the odds, or a community coming together in the face of hardship, these stories serve as reminders of what is possible with determination, courage, and perseverance. When you immerse yourself in such stories, you may find new perspectives on your own struggles, igniting a sense of hope and motivation to pursue your goals.

Practice Self-Talk

Encourage yourself with positive words

Practicing self-talk is a vital tool for cultivating a positive mindset and nurturing your self-esteem. The way you speak to yourself can significantly influence your thoughts, feelings, and actions. By consciously choosing to encourage yourself with positive words, you create a supportive inner dialogue that fosters resilience and motivation. Instead of allowing negative thoughts to take hold, replace them with affirmations that reinforce your strengths and capabilities—statements like "I am gifted," "I am worthy," or "I can overcome challenges." This simple yet powerful practice not only helps you navigate difficult moments with greater ease but also builds a foundation of self-compassion and confidence. As you become more attuned to your self-talk, you empower yourself to face obstacles with a constructive attitude, turning self-doubt into self-encouragement. Make this a regular practice and see your life change.

Organize Your Workspace

A clean space sharpens focus

A clean and clutter-free environment allows your mind to concentrate on the tasks at hand without distraction. When you take the time to declutter your desk, arrange your stuff, you create a space for creativity and efficiency. You find what you need easily, minimizing the stress associated with a chaotic environment. Moreover, a well-organized workspace creates a sense of accomplishments and readiness, preparing you mentally for the challenges ahead. By prioritizing the organization of your workspace, you set the stage for increased focus, clarity, and motivation, ultimately leading to a more productive and fulfilling day.

Plan a Healthy Lunch

Give yourself energy for the day

Planning a healthy lunch is a key strategy for fuelling your body and mind, providing you with the energy you need to power through the day. By taking the time to prepare balanced meals that include a variety of nutrients—such as lean proteins, whole grains, fresh vegetables, and healthy fats—you not only nourish your body but also support your overall well-being. A well-planned lunch can help maintain stable blood sugar levels, preventing the afternoon slump that often leads to fatigue and decreased productivity. By prioritizing a healthy lunch, you cultivate mindful eating habits and make a conscious effort to care for yourself, setting a positive tone for the rest of your day.

Say No to Snooze

Resist snoozing to get up fresh

Saying no to the snooze button is a powerful practice that can set a positive tone for your entire day. While it may be tempting to indulge in those extra few minutes of sleep, hitting snooze often leads to grogginess and disrupts your natural sleep cycle. By resisting the urge to snooze, you train your body to wake up with intention, allowing you to rise and shine feeling refreshed and alert. Consider placing your alarm clock across the room, so you have to physically get up to turn it off. This small change can help you break the snooze habit and cultivate a more refreshing start to your day.

Try Progressive Muscle Relaxation

Bonding with animals can boost mood

Trying progressive muscle relaxation (PMR) is an effective technique for relieving stress and promoting a sense of calm and well-being. This practice involves systematically tensing and then relaxing different muscle groups in your body, helping you become more aware of physical tension and its release. Start by finding a quiet space where you can sit or lie down comfortably. Begin at your toes, tensing the muscles for a few seconds before letting go and feeling the relaxation that follows. Gradually work your way up through your legs, abdomen, arms, and face, focusing on each muscle group in turn. As you practice PMR, you will notice a profound sense of relaxation as tension dissipates, leaving you feeling lighter and more cantered. This method not only helps to alleviate physical discomfort but also fosters mental clarity by promoting mindfulness. This is a powerful tool for managing stress and enhancing your overall well-being.

Visualize Your Best Self

Picture yourself in a successful state

By taking a moment to close your eyes and imagine yourself in a successful state, you engage your mind in a powerful exercise of intention and motivation. Picture every detail: how you look, how you carry yourself, and the feelings of confidence and accomplishment that accompany your success. This mental imagery serves as a guiding force, helping you align your actions with your aspirations. Visualization can reinforce your self-belief, making it easier to navigate challenges and setbacks, as you have a clear image of what you are working toward. Incorporating this practice into your daily routine allows you to tap into the positive emotions associated with your achievements, fostering a sense of purpose and direction. By regularly visualizing your best self, you create a roadmap for success, inspiring you to take the necessary steps to turn your dreams into reality.

Step Outside

Nature's serenity boosts mood

Stepping outside and immersing yourself in nature is a simple yet profound way to boost your mood and enhance your overall well-being. The tranquillity of the natural world offers a refreshing escape from the hustle and bustle of daily life, allowing you to reconnect with your surroundings and find peace. Whether it is a walk in the park, a stroll through a garden, or just sitting under a tree, being outdoors can lower stress levels and improve your mental clarity. Exposure to natural light increases serotonin production, a neurotransmitter that contributes to feelings of happiness and well-being. Additionally, the sounds of chirping birds, rustling leaves, and flowing water can have a calming effect on your mind, further elevating your mood. Taking time to step outside not only revitalizes your spirit but also reminds you of the beauty and wonder of the world around you. By making it a daily habit, you cultivate a greater appreciation for nature and create moments of joy and serenity that can carry you through the rest of your day.

Try Brain Training Apps

Challenge your cognitive skills

Trying brain training apps is an engaging way to challenge and enhance your cognitive skills while making learning enjoyable. These interactive applications offer a variety of exercises designed to stimulate different areas of your brain, including memory, attention, problem-solving, and critical thinking. By incorporating these games into your daily routine, you can improve your mental agility and boost your overall brain health. Many brain training apps also provide personalized feedback, allowing you to track your progress and set achievable goals. As you challenge yourself with new tasks and puzzles, you will find that your ability to think creatively and adapt to complex situations improves, enhancing your everyday problem-solving skills and enriching your overall mental well-being.

Plan Intentional Downtime

Schedule breaks for well-being

Planning intentional downtime is essential for maintaining your well-being and enhancing overall productivity. In our fast-paced world, it is easy to get caught up in the whirlwind of tasks and responsibilities, often neglecting the importance of taking breaks. By deliberately scheduling time for relaxation and rejuvenation, you create opportunities to recharge your mind and body. Whether it is a short walk outside, reading a book, or simply sitting in silence, these moments of downtime allow you to step back, reflect, and refocus. Incorporating breaks into your daily routine can reduce stress levels, improve concentration, and boost creativity, ultimately leading to more effective and efficient work.

Clean Your Phone Screen

A small action for a clear mind

Cleaning your phone screen is a small but impactful action that can lead to a clearer mind and a more focused day. Our phones are often the primary tools we use for communication, productivity, and entertainment, and a smudged or cluttered screen can serve as a constant distraction. By taking a moment to wipe away fingerprints or dust creates a more inviting and organized digital workspace. This simple task can help reduce visual clutter, making it easier to navigate your apps and notifications. Furthermore, a clean phone screen can symbolize a fresh start, reinforcing the idea of tidying up both your physical and mental space.

Review a Core Value

Align your actions with values

Reviewing a core value is a powerful practice that allows you to align your actions with your beliefs, nurturing a sense of integrity and purpose in your life. Taking the time to reflect on what truly matters to you—whether it is honesty, compassion, growth, or another guiding principle—helps you evaluate your decisions and behaviours in light of these values. This process of introspection encourages you to ask important questions: Are my daily actions reflecting my core values? Am I living authentically? By identifying any discrepancies between your values and your actions, you can make conscious adjustments that lead to a more fulfilling and harmonious life.

Practice Stillness

Start with five quiet minutes

Practicing stillness is a transformative practice that can significantly enhance your mental clarity and emotional well-being. Starting with just five quiet minutes each day allows you to cultivate a sense of peace and presence in an often chaotic world. Find a comfortable space where you can sit or lie down without distractions. Close your eyes, take a few deep breaths, and allow yourself to simply be in the moment. Focus on your breath or the sensations in your body, gently redirecting your mind whenever it starts to wander. This small investment of time can help quiet the noise of daily life, providing an opportunity to recharge and reflect. As you make stillness a habit, you may find it easier to manage stress, improve your concentration, and foster a greater sense of calm. Over time, these five minutes can evolve into a cherished ritual, offering you the clarity and tranquillity needed to approach the rest of your day with intention and purpose. This practice also brings you to the present moment.

Laugh

It is indeed the best medicine

Laughing is a joyful and powerful way to lighten your mood and relieve stress. Taking the time to watch something funny—be it a comedy show, a hilarious movie, or a series of funny clips—can evoke laughter that uplifts your spirit and creates a sense of connection with others. Laughter triggers the release of endorphins, the body's natural feel-good chemicals, which can boost your overall sense of happiness and well-being. It also serves as a wonderful reminder to not take life too seriously, helping to shift your perspective during challenging times. Whether you are sharing a laugh with friends or enjoying a moment of silliness on your own, humour has the remarkable ability to bring joy and lighten the weight of daily pressures. Laughter is a simple yet effective way to brighten your day and rejuvenate your spirit.

Read an Inspiring Biography

A clean space sharpens focus

Reading an inspiring biography is a powerful way to learn from the journeys of successful individuals and draw motivation from their experiences. Biographies offer unique insights into the lives of people who have overcome challenges, pursued their passions, and achieved great things. By exploring their stories, you can gain valuable lessons about resilience, perseverance, and the importance of staying true to one's values. Whether it's a celebrated leader, an artist, an entrepreneur, or an activist, each biography provides a glimpse into the obstacles faced and the strategies employed to navigate life's ups and downs. These narratives serve as sources of inspiration and as you read about their triumphs and failures, you may find parallels to your own life. Making this a part of your daily routine will ignite the spark in you and motivate you to move towards your goals.

Organize a Vision Board

Keep your dreams in sight

Organizing a vision board is a creative and empowering way to keep your dreams and aspirations in front of you. Reinforce your intentions by surrounding yourself with images, words, and symbols that resonate with your ambitions. Start by gathering materials like magazines, printouts, or art supplies, and set aside time to reflect on what you truly want to achieve. As you curate your vision board, include elements that inspire you—whether they are images of places you want to visit, quotes that motivate you, or representations of personal milestones you wish to reach. Placing your completed vision board in a visible spot serves as a constant reminder of your goals, helping to keep you focused and motivated. This enhances your commitment to your dreams and allows you to visualize your success, making it feel more within your reach.

Review What's Not Essential

Simplify your goals

In a world filled with distractions and cut-throat competition, it is easy to become overwhelmed by an endless to-do list that detracts from your core objectives. By taking the time to evaluate your commitments and aspirations, you can identify tasks and goals that no longer align with your values or long-term vision. This process encourages you to let go of what is unnecessary, freeing up mental and emotional space to concentrate on your essential goals. Consider asking yourself which activities bring you joy, fulfilment, or progress, and which ones feel like obligations or sources of stress. Simplifying your goals allows you to streamline your efforts and prioritize your energy on what truly contributes to your growth and happiness.

Practice Self-Reflection

Identify strengths and areas to grow

Practicing self-reflection is a crucial process for personal growth and development, allowing you to gain insights into your strengths and areas for improvement. By taking time to pause and examine your thoughts, feelings, and behaviours, you cultivate a deeper understanding of yourself and your experiences. Start by setting aside a few quiet moments to reflect on recent events, interactions, or challenges you've faced. Consider questions such as: What went well? What challenges did I encounter? How did I handle them? By identifying your strengths—whether they be resilience, creativity, or effective communication—you can celebrate your accomplishments and build on these positive attributes. Simultaneously, recognizing areas for growth provides you with a roadmap for self-improvement, guiding your future efforts and setting meaningful goals. Incorporating self-reflection into your routine fosters a mindset of continuous learning and adaptation, allowing you to evolve as a person.

Draw a Mind Map

Visualize ideas or tasks

Drawing a mind map is an effective and creative way to visualize ideas or tasks, helping you to organize your thoughts and enhance your understanding of complex topics. This graphical representation allows you to break down information into manageable components, making it easier to see relationships and connections between different concepts. To create a mind map, start with a central idea or theme in the middle of a blank page, and branch out with related topics or tasks, using lines or arrows to connect them. You can incorporate colours, images, and keywords to make the mind map visually appealing and more memorable. This technique encourages free-flowing ideas by engaging both the left and right hemispheres of your brain. Whether you are planning a project, outlining a chapter for a book, or simply trying to organize your thoughts, mind mapping can help clarify your objectives and streamline your focus.

Review Your Schedule

Plan your day to avoid surprises

Reviewing your schedule is an essential practice that helps you plan your day effectively and minimize unexpected surprises. By taking a few moments each morning or the night before to examine your calendar, you gain clarity on your commitments, priorities, and available time. This proactive approach allows you to allocate your energy and resources more wisely, ensuring that you tackle important tasks without feeling rushed or overwhelmed.

Find Your Focus Item

A small object can help you centre

Finding your focus item is a simple yet effective technique to help center your thoughts and enhance your concentration. A focus item can be any small object—a stone, a pen, a piece of jewellery, or even a stress ball—that resonates with you and serves as a tangible reminder of your intentions and goals. By keeping this object within reach, you can use it as a focal point during moments of distraction or overwhelm. Whenever you find your mind wandering or your energy scattered, take a moment to hold the item, observe its details, and breathe deeply. This act grounds you in the present moment and reinforces your commitment to staying focused on your tasks or objectives. Additionally, associating your focus item with specific feelings or affirmations can enhance its effectiveness, making it a powerful tool for mindfulness.

Take Three Deep Breaths

Reset your focus

Taking three deep breaths is a simple yet powerful technique to reset your focus and regain clarity in moments of stress or distraction. When you pause to breathe deeply, you activate your body's relaxation response, signaling to your mind that it's time to slow down and refocus. Start by inhaling deeply through your nose, allowing your abdomen to expand fully, and then exhale slowly through your mouth, letting go of any tension or distractions. Repeat this process three times, concentrating on the rhythm of your breath and the sensations in your body. With each inhalation, visualize drawing in calmness and clarity, and with each exhalation, imagine releasing stress and mental clutter. This practice not only helps to centre your thoughts but also improves your overall well-being by increasing oxygen flow to your brain, enhancing your cognitive function.

Practice Kindness

Think of a way to show kindness today

Practicing kindness is a beautiful way to brighten your day and the days of those around you. Start by reflecting on simple gestures that can make a meaningful impact, such as complimenting a colleague, helping a neighbour with their groceries, or sending a thoughtful message to a friend. Acts of kindness can be as small as holding the door open for someone or offering a genuine smile to a stranger, creating ripples of goodwill in your community. These acts encourage empathy and connection, making this world a better place. Moreover, kindness has a remarkable way of enhancing our mental well-being, as it enriches our lives and of those around us.

Pray for Someone in Need

Praying for others opens your heart

Praying for someone is a profound and selfless gesture that extends love, hope, and compassion beyond ourselves. When we take a moment to lift someone else's needs, struggles, or dreams to a higher power, we connect with them on a deeply spiritual level. This act of prayer is not only beneficial for the person being prayed for, but it also nurtures empathy and kindness within us. Whether we are praying for a loved one's health, a friend's success, or even a stranger's peace, we send positive energy and support into their lives, often offering solace and strength in ways words alone cannot. Praying for others reminds us of the power of unity and compassion, and it opens our hearts to the interconnectedness of humanity, fostering a sense of peace and fulfilment within.

Connect with a Mentor

Reach out for inspiration

Connecting with a mentor can open doors to insights and inspiration you never knew you needed. A good mentor isn't just a guide—there are the ones who have travelled the path you're on and know a few shortcuts. Whether you are looking to level up in your career, gain new skills, or make big life choices, reaching out to someone you admire can spark fresh ideas and bring new clarity. Start with a friendly message or casual coffee chat, and come ready with questions that show you are excited to learn. This simple step can lead to eye-opening advice, boost your confidence, and expand your network, helping you move closer to the life you're aiming for.

Focus on the Present

Ground yourself in "here and now"

Focusing on the present moment is a vital practice that helps ground you in the "here and now," promoting a sense of clarity and peace amid life's distractions. When your mind drifts to the past or worries about the future, it can create feelings of anxiety and overwhelm. By consciously directing your attention to the present, you cultivate mindfulness, allowing you to fully experience and appreciate each moment. Start by taking a few deep breaths to anchor yourself, paying attention to the sensations in your body and the environment around you. Notice the sounds, smells, and textures that are present—this sensory awareness helps to pull you into the moment. Engaging in activities such as meditation, mindful walking, or simply savouring a meal can deepen your connection to the present. Practicing gratitude for what you have right now enhances this experience, reminding you of the abundance in your life. By focusing on the present, you reduce stress and increase your overall well-being, enabling you to approach challenges with a clearer mind and a more open heart.

Practice Self-Love

Give yourself positive affirmations

Practicing self-love is an essential aspect of nurturing a healthy relationship with yourself, and one powerful way to cultivate this love is through positive affirmations. These affirmations are simple, positive statements that reinforce your worth, capabilities, and strengths. By regularly repeating affirmations such as "I am complete in all respects," "I invite all the good things in my life," or "I am worthy of love," you create a nurturing inner dialogue that combats negative self-talk and self-doubt. Start your day by choosing a few affirmations that resonate with you, and say them aloud or write them down in a journal. As you engage with these statements, allow yourself to feel the truth in them, embracing the positive energy they bring. This practice not only enhances your self-esteem but also helps you develop a more compassionate and forgiving attitude toward yourself. Incorporating self-love into your daily routine promotes emotional well-being and empowers you to take on day's challenges in your stride.

Start with a Challenge

Complete a difficult task early

Starting your day with a challenge by completing a difficult task early can set a powerful tone for the rest of your day. Tackling a significant challenge first thing in the morning not only boosts your productivity but also enhances your confidence and motivation. When you prioritize a tough task, such as a complex project or an important meeting, you take advantage of your fresh energy and mental clarity after a good night's rest. This proactive approach can help you overcome procrastination and reduce anxiety, as you eliminate a source of stress right at the start.

Simplify Your Outfit Choice

Limit decisions to reduce stress

Simplifying your outfit choice each morning is a small but effective way to reduce decision fatigue and start the day with a clear mind. By limiting the choices, you make for what to wear, you conserve mental energy for the more important decisions and tasks ahead. Many successful people, from CEOs to creatives, embrace this habit, often by curating a capsule wardrobe or choosing a "uniform" of favourite go-to pieces. This approach not only minimizes stress but also streamlines your morning routine, allowing you to focus on what truly matters. Choosing an outfit quickly and with confidence means one less thing to worry about, giving you a sense of control and readiness as you step into your day. Over time, this small adjustment can have a big impact, enabling you to start each morning with more focus and peace.

Think of Your Loved Ones

Strengthens motivation and purpose

Taking a moment to think of your loved ones is a powerful way to reinforce your motivation and sense of purpose. Reflecting on the people who support, encourage, and inspire you can reignite your drive, especially during challenging times. Loved ones—whether family, friends, or mentors—often represent our "why" for striving toward our goals, pushing us to work harder and become the best versions of ourselves. By visualizing their smiles, recalling a shared memory, or even considering how your actions impact them, you can feel a renewed sense of determination, focus and positivity.

Appreciate a Simple Moment

Mindfully observe your surroundings

Appreciating a simple moment invites you to pause, breathe, and mindfully connect with your surroundings, fostering a sense of calm and gratitude. Whether it's noticing the warmth of sunlight filtering through a window, feeling the gentle breeze on your face, or simply enjoying the aroma of your morning coffee, these small moments offer a chance to slow down and reconnect with the present. By fully immersing yourself in these experiences, you give your mind a break from the rush of daily tasks and worries. Take a moment to observe without judgment, noticing textures, colours, sounds, or sensations, and allow yourself to feel grounded in the here and now. Practicing this regularly can enhance your mood, reduce stress, and remind you of the beauty in everyday life. Ultimately, appreciating a simple moment nurtures mindfulness and gratitude, enriching your day with a renewed sense of peace and awareness.

Start Small for Big Wins

Focus on a tiny habit or goal

Starting small is a powerful strategy for achieving big wins, allowing you to build momentum with manageable, bite-sized habits or goals. When you focus on a tiny habit—such as drinking a glass of water each morning, setting aside five minutes for meditation, or writing one line in a journal—you create a routine that is easy to maintain, yet has the potential to snowball into lasting change. Small, achievable actions help bypass the overwhelm that often accompanies big goals, making it more likely that you'll stick with them over time. As these small habits become second nature, you'll notice a ripple effect; the confidence and sense of accomplishment you gain from sticking to these "wins" will inspire you to take on bigger challenges. By starting small, you create a sustainable foundation for growth, transforming tiny efforts into meaningful progress that ultimately leads to significant, lasting achievements.

List Your Accomplishments

Limit decisions to reduce stress

Listing your accomplishments is a powerful way to boost confidence and remind yourself of your capabilities. Taking a few moments to reflect on past wins, whether big or small, allows you to see just how far you've come and reinforces a positive mindset. By acknowledging these successes, you build self-belief, which can be especially valuable when facing new challenges or setting future goals. Start by writing down achievements that come to you mind—these could be work-related milestones, personal growth moments, or acts of kindness and resilience. This exercise not only strengthens your self-worth but also motivates you to keep striving, knowing that you are capable of great things. Keeping an "accomplishments list" that you can revisit can provide an extra boost on tough days, serving as a reminder of your strengths and the progress you have made.

Focus on Small Pleasures

Savor tiny joys

Focusing on small pleasures allows you to slow down and appreciate the tiny joys that make each day meaningful. These simple moments—a warm cup of tea, the sound of rain, the laughter of a loved one, or the feel of soft fabric—are easy to overlook in the busyness of life, yet they hold immense power to uplift our mood and reconnect us to the present. Taking time to appreciate these small delights reminds us that happiness isn't only found in big milestones but also in the everyday beauty surrounding us. When you consciously notice and savour these moments, you cultivate gratitude and contentment, making it easier to navigate challenges with a grounded, joyful spirit. Embracing small pleasures as part of your routine can enhance your well-being and enrich your perspective, helping you find beauty in the ordinary.

Let go and move on

Don't be the prisoners of your past

Letting go and moving on is a courageous act of self-liberation that opens the door to healing and new beginnings. When we hold onto past hurts, regrets, or relationships that no longer serve us, we inadvertently anchor ourselves to a place of stagnation, blocking growth and peace. Releasing what weighs us down can feel daunting, as it often involves confronting painful memories or accepting what's out of our control. Yet, letting go doesn't mean forgetting or dismissing the past; it means choosing to no longer let it define us or our future. Moving on allows us to reclaim our energy and focus it on creating a life that aligns with our present values and aspirations. In this way, letting go becomes an act of self-compassion, giving ourselves permission to heal, grow, and embrace the opportunities that lie ahead. So every morning, filter your thoughts and let go of the ones that hold no good for your future.

Give Yourself Grace

You are allowed to go slow sometimes

Giving yourself grace is a gentle reminder that it is okay to go slow and take things one step at a time. Life often pressures us to keep pushing forward at full speed, but allowing yourself moments to pause, reset, or move at a slower pace can be incredibly healing. Embracing self-compassion means accepting that you are human, with limits, and that it is perfectly normal to have days where you need extra time or space to recharge. By giving yourself grace, you create room for rest, reflection, and growth, honouring your journey without judgment. This practice nurtures resilience and self-respect, reinforcing that your worth is not defined by productivity alone. Embrace the freedom to ease up, knowing that some of the most meaningful progress happens when you allow yourself to simply be.

Play with Colours

Use art supplies or reorganize colours

Playing with colours is a refreshing way to spark creativity and lift your mood. Whether you're doodling with markers, experimenting with paint, or simply reorganizing items by colour, this simple activity can bring a sense of joy and relaxation. Colours have the power to influence our emotions—bright shades can energize, cool tones can calm, and rich hues can inspire. Grab a set of coloured pencils, pens, or even a colouring book, and let yourself explore without worrying about perfection. If art supplies aren't handy, try organizing your space by colour, like arranging books on shelf or sorting clothes in your wardrobe. Engaging with colours can serve as a form of mindfulness, focusing your attention on the here and now. This playful practice encourages self-expression and adds a splash of vibrancy to your day, reminding you of the beauty in simple, colourful moments.

Track Progress

Notice how far you have come

Tracking your progress is a meaningful way to acknowledge and celebrate how far you have come. When you take the time to reflect on your journey, you see the small victories, the lessons learned, and the steps that have brought you closer to your goals. By writing down milestones, noting challenges overcome, or even snapping photos of key moments, you create a visible record of your efforts. This practice not only builds confidence but also reinforces motivation, helping you stay focused and encouraged on tough days. Remember, progress isn't always linear—it's often a series of small steps and occasional setbacks. By regularly checking in on your growth, you remind yourself of your resilience and commitment, creating a positive feedback loop that keeps you moving forward with gratitude and pride.

Look at Photos

Limit decisions to reduce stress

Looking at photos is a wonderful way to boost your mood and reconnect with positive memories. Each image serves as a visual reminder of joyful moments, cherished experiences, and the people who have brought happiness into your life. Whether it is a snapshot from a memorable vacation, a family gathering, or a candid shot with friends, these photos can evoke feelings of nostalgia, warmth, and gratitude. Taking a few moments to browse through your collection allows you to relive those special times and appreciate the beauty of your journey. This simple act can create an instant uplift in your spirits, reminding you of the love and joy that surround you. Incorporating a photo review into your routine can serve as a delightful pick-me-up, helping to cultivate a positive mindset and reinforcing the connections that enrich your life.

Practice Acceptance

Embrace where you are right now

Practicing acceptance involves embracing your current situation, acknowledging it without judgment, and recognizing that it's okay to be exactly where you are. Life can be unpredictable, and it is common to feel a sense of resistance when faced with challenges or uncertainty. However, acceptance allows you to let go of the need to control everything and fosters a sense of peace amidst the chaos. By accepting your present circumstances—whether they are good, bad, or somewhere in between—you create space for growth, healing, and new opportunities. This practice encourages self-compassion, reminding you that it's okay to have difficult feelings and that every experience contributes to your journey. Embracing where you are right now not only alleviates stress but also opens your heart to possibilities, helping you move forward with a clearer mind and a lighter spirit.

Review a Life Goal

Keeps you connected to a bigger picture

Reviewing a life goal is a powerful practice that helps you stay connected to the bigger picture of your aspirations and dreams. By taking the time to reflect on your long-term objectives, you reinforce your sense of purpose and direction, reminding yourself of what truly matters to you. This process encourages you to evaluate your progress, identify any obstacles, and celebrate the milestones you've achieved along the way. It also provides an opportunity to reassess your goals, ensuring they still align with your values and vision for the future.

Forgive

Don't be too harsh on yourself

Forgiveness is an important practice that encourages you to let go of self-criticism and the weight of past mistakes. It is essential to remember that everyone makes errors, and being too harsh on yourself can hinder your growth and well-being. When you forgive yourself, you acknowledge your humanity and accept that imperfections are part of the journey. This act of compassion allows you to release feelings of guilt or shame, paving the way for healing and personal growth. Instead of dwelling on what went wrong, focus on the lessons learned and how they can inform your future choices. Practicing self-forgiveness not only cultivates a healthier relationship with yourself but also fosters resilience, enabling you to move forward with a clearer mind and an open heart. By choosing to forgive, you empower yourself to embrace new opportunities and live more fully in the present.

Dress to Kill

Dress the best possible way

"Dressing to kill" is more than just putting on clothes; it is about wearing what makes you feel confident, empowered, and ready to take on the world. When you choose an outfit that reflects your style and makes you feel your best, you not only enhance your appearance but also elevate your mood and self-esteem. Whether it is a sharp suit, a stunning dress, or your favourite casual ensemble, the right attire can act as a form of armour, giving you the confidence to navigate any situation. Dressing well allows you to express your personality and can make a significant impact on how others perceive you. It is a reminder that taking the time to curate your look shows respect for yourself and the environment you are in. So, embrace the art of dressing to kill; it's not just about looking good—it's about feeling unstoppable and ready to shine!

Celebrate Your Wins

Small or big, acknowledge your progress

Celebrating your wins, whether big or small, is an essential practice for nurturing a positive mindset and maintaining motivation. Acknowledging your achievements helps reinforce your sense of self-worth and encourages you to keep striving toward your goals. When you take the time to celebrate, you create a moment of joy and reflection, allowing yourself to fully appreciate the effort and dedication you have put in. This could be as simple as treating yourself to a favourite snack, sharing your success with friends, or taking a moment to write down what you have accomplished. Celebrating wins fosters a culture of gratitude and positivity in your life, reminding you that every step forward is worth recognizing. By making this practice a habit, you not only build resilience but also cultivate a greater appreciation for your journey, ultimately empowering you to face future challenges with confidence and enthusiasm.

Morning Habits of successful people

Benjamin Franklin

Benjamin Franklin, one of the founding fathers of the United States, was a remarkable figure known for his diverse roles as a scientist, author, activist, and more. Despite his many responsibilities, Franklin placed a high value on self-improvement and personal growth.

He meticulously designed a strict daily routine, allocating specific times for sleeping, meals, work, and other activities. Franklin even created a detailed chart outlining his hourly tasks. What truly set his routine apart, however, was his commitment to reflection and purpose. Each morning, he would begin his day by asking himself, *"What good shall I do this day?"* and conclude it with the reflective question, *"What good have I done today?"*

Barack Obama

During his time as President of the United States, Barack Obama maintained a daily routine that he followed diligently. Every morning, he had breakfast with his wife, Michelle, and their daughters, Malia and Sasha. He also helped his daughters get ready for school. His mornings included reading newspapers and exercising, which typically involved weights and cardio, before starting his workday in the Oval Office around 9 a.m.

Obama prioritized having dinner with his family each evening before returning to work, often staying as late as 10 p.m. He was also careful to minimize distractions and decision fatigue, as he shared in an interview: *"I don't want to make decisions about what I'm eating or wearing because I have too many other decisions to make."*

Despite the immense pressures of the presidency, Obama's solid routine helped him balance his responsibilities and maintain time for family, health, and work effectively.

Evan Clark Williams

During his time as President of the United States, Evan Clark Williams, an American computer programmer and Internet entrepreneur, is the founder of influential platforms like Blogger, Twitter, and Medium. As a former chairman and CEO of Twitter, one of the world's most visited websites, one might assume that Williams spends all his waking hours immersed in work. However, he prioritizes taking a mid-day break to visit the gym.

Williams believes it's important to understand how individual energy levels fluctuate throughout the day to maximize productivity. While he once worked out in the mornings, he realized that this wasn't the best time for him. *"My focus is usually great first thing in the morning, so going to the gym first is a trade-off of a very productive time. Instead, I've started going mid-morning or late afternoon, especially on days I work late,"* he explains.

By adjusting his schedule and incorporating gym sessions later in the day, Williams has found a routine that better supports his energy levels, productivity, and overall well-being.

Steve Jobs

Steve Jobs, the former Apple CEO, was known for his passion, focus, and simplicity, which helped transform Apple into the world's most valuable company. To stay motivated, he started every morning with a personal reflection. Standing in front of a mirror, he would ask himself: *"If today were the last day of my life, would I be happy with what I'm about to do today?"*

If the answer was "no" for too many days in a row, Jobs knew it was time for a change. His famous quote encapsulates his philosophy:

"Your time is limited, so don't waste it living someone else's life. Don't be trapped by dogma – which is living with the results of other people's thinking. Don't let the noise of others' opinions drown out your own inner voice. And most important, have the courage to follow your heart and intuition."

By beginning his day with this simple yet profound question, Jobs ensured he was always taking steps toward a meaningful and successful life.

Oprah Winfrey

Oprah Winfrey, one of the most influential celebrities in the world, attributes much of her strength and success to her practice of spending 20 minutes in stillness twice a day. Despite enduring unimaginable hardships—including child abuse, poverty, and trauma—Oprah emerged as a beacon of inspiration for millions.

She credits her stillness practice for her resilience, saying, *"This practice induces hope, a sense of contentment, and deep joy. Knowing for sure that even in the daily craziness that bombards us from every direction, there is still the constancy of stillness. Only from that space can you create your best work and your best life."*

For Oprah, those 20 minutes of stillness serve as a grounding force, enabling her to navigate life with grace and purpose while setting the tone for a productive and fulfilling day.

Howard Schultz

Howard Schultz, the former CEO of Starbucks, begins his day at 4:30 a.m. with a walk with his three dogs. This morning ritual sets a calm and active tone for his day.

By 5:45 a.m., Schultz is back home, preparing coffee for himself and his wife. Known for his attention to detail, he prefers a "coarse grind of aged Sumatra," steeped in boiling water for exactly 3-4 minutes—a testament to his appreciation for quality and craftsmanship.

This combination of early exercise, family time, and his passion for coffee fuels his energy and focus before he transitions to work.

Jennifer Aniston

Jennifer Aniston, the beloved star of Friends, follows a disciplined morning routine that contributes to her radiant appearance and peaceful mind. She starts her day at 4:30 a.m. with a glass of hot water and lemon, followed by washing her face with soap and water. She then spends 20 minutes meditating, centering herself for the day ahead.

For breakfast, Aniston opts for a protein shake before heading to her personal trainer for an intense workout. Her routine includes 30 minutes of spin, 40 minutes of yoga, and additional time at the gym—a regimen that keeps her body fit, her skin glowing, and her mind at peace.

Jeff Bezos

Jeff Bezos, the founder of Amazon, takes a more relaxed approach to his mornings. He avoids early meetings and instead prioritizes spending quality time with his wife and children at the breakfast table. This unhurried start helps him maintain a healthy work-life balance and reduces stress.

By dedicating his mornings to family and leisure, Bezos ensures he is in the right frame of mind to tackle the day's challenges with focus and productivity.

Richard Branson

Richard Branson, the founder of the Virgin Group, is a firm believer in starting the day early. Rising at 5 a.m., Branson uses the early hours to exercise and spend time with his family.

As he shared in a blog post, *"I'm able to do some exercise and spend time with my family, which puts me in a great mind frame before getting down to business."*

This early morning routine helps him stay energized and positive, setting the tone for a productive and successful day ahead.

Conclusion

As you reach the end of *Morning Mastery:101 morning habits to transform your day*, I hope you have discovered valuable insights, simple practices, and inspiring ideas to bring more vitality, focus, and joy into your mornings. Each of these tips serves as a small but powerful tool to help you take control of your day from the moment you wake up, transforming your mornings into a purposeful ritual that empowers you to live fully.

Creating a morning routine that works for you is a deeply personal journey, and it is perfectly okay if only a handful of these suggestions resonate with you. The key is to find what fits naturally into your life, aligns with your goals, and nurtures your well-being. Remember, sustainable change doesn't come from rigid routines or perfection but from consistent, mindful efforts that feel rewarding and authentic.

By now, you have seen the potential of intentional mornings—not just to improve productivity, but to enhance mental clarity, elevate mood, and deepen your connection to yourself. Morning by morning, these small actions add up, shaping the way you experience each day and helping you cultivate a mindset that fosters resilience and fulfilment.

So, take what you have learned here and make it a practice. Keep experimenting, adjusting, and evolving your routine as life shifts and your needs change. Let your mornings be a time to set your intentions, honour your health, and nourish your spirit. With each new day, you have the chance to create a fresh start and make choices that empower you to live with purpose.

Here's to embracing each morning as an opportunity to grow, thrive, and create a life that reflects your dreams and aspirations. Wishing you many energizing, inspiring mornings ahead!

Cheers!

Aruna Joshi is a passionate writer and currently leads the Editorial department of a renowned publishing house in Mumbai. Her expertise lies in spirituality, self-help, and personal growth, areas where her work has inspired countless readers.

Aruna graduated with a degree in Architecture in 1993 and practiced the profession for 18 years. However, her true calling emerged in writing, a passion she has now wholeheartedly embraced.

A creative genius, as many of her friends fondly describe her, Aruna has explored various artistic fields throughout her life. She is an accomplished painter, designer, and artist who received much praise for her work. Yet, despite her success in the arts, her heart consistently gravitated toward writing—a love that had been quietly present since childhood.

Her first foray into writing came at the age of

12 when she penned a set of poems. This initial experience marked the beginning of her journey, sparking a sense of liberation and joy in expressing her thoughts through words. After completing her education, she briefly worked for an architectural magazine, further nurturing her love for writing.

Aruna has contributed to numerous books on spirituality and personal growth, and her articles have been featured in leading Mind-Body-Soul magazines. She also shares her wisdom through regular blog posts, connecting with readers on a deeply personal level.

A deeply creative and passionate soul, Aruna pours her heart into every endeavour. Her writing is infused with spiritual wisdom and is characterized by its simplicity and relatability. Through real-life examples, she conveys her messages effectively, making her books engaging and impactful for readers of all ages. Her work motivates and inspires people to embrace positive change, making her a beacon of encouragement and hope in the world of self-help and personal growth.

Aruna Joshi has authored three books: *Wake Up - Morning Rituals for a Productive and Successful Day*, *The Happiness Manual*, and *The Subtle Art of Dealing with People*. Following the tremendous success of *Wake Up*, Aruna was inspired to transform its simple, effective concepts into 101 nuggets, allowing readers to actively apply her teachings and enhance their daily lives.

NOTES

NOTES

NOTES

NOTES

NOTES